Before and After

EASTER

Activities and Ideas for Lent to Pentecost

D1450858

By Debbie Trafton O'Neal
Illustrated by David LaRochelle

Augsburg
MINNEAPOLIS

From my family to yours—

*May the season of Lent be a time of
reflection and renewal for you,
and may Easter morning fill your hearts
with joy that lasts throughout the year!*

BEFORE AND AFTER EASTER
Activities and Ideas for Lent to Pentecost

Scripture quotations unless otherwise noted are from the *Holy Bible, New International Version.*® Copyright © 1973, 1978, 1984 by International Bible Society. Used by permission of Zondervan Publishing House. All rights reserved. The "NIV" and "New International Version" trademarks are registered in the United States Patent and Trademark Office by International Bible Society. Use of either trademark requires the permission of International Bible Society.

The activities on pages 6, 54, and 55 are from *An Easter People: Family Devotional Activities for Lent and Easter* by Debbie Trafton O'Neal, copyright © 1986 Augsburg Publishing House.

The Lord's Prayer activity on page 15 is from *God's People Pray*, Grades 3-4 Student Pack (1985 Vacation Bible School), copyright © 1984 Augsburg Publishing House.

The five-finger prayer activity on page 18 is from *More Than Glue and Glitter: A Classroom Guide for Volunteer Teachers* by Debbie Trafton O'Neal, copyright © 1992 Augsburg Fortress.

Library of Congress Cataloging-in-Publication Data

O'Neal, Debbie Trafton.
    Before and after Easter : activities and ideas for Lent to Pentecost / by Debbie Trafton O'Neal : illustrated by David LaRochelle.
        p. cm.
    ISBN 0-8066-2604-6 :
    1. Lent. 2. Easter. 3. Pentecost. 4. Family—Religious life. 5. Activity programs in Christian education.   I. LaRochelle, David. II. Title.
BV85.049 1992
263'.9—dc20   92-32415
                                                           CIP

The paper used in this publication meets the minimum requirements of American National Standard for Information Sciences—Permanence of Paper for Printed Library Materials, ANSI Z329.48-1984. ∞™

Manufactured in the U.S.A.   AF 9-2604

10

HOW TO USE THIS BOOK

The season of Lent in the church year is perhaps one of the most important and significant to God's people. Just as Advent is a time for preparing our lives for the coming of Christ at Christmas, so Lent can help us prepare for celebrating the joyful message of the resurrection at Easter and for welcoming the coming of the Holy Spirit as it came to the apostles on the Day of Pentecost.

This book is intended primarily for use by families, but anyone will find much of interest here, especially those who work with children. It contains information about the history and traditions of the seasons of Lent, Easter, and Pentecost, as well as symbols and their meanings, the stories and legends of the seasons, and activities for the days of Lent and the weeks between Easter and the Day of Pentecost.

Read through the entire book to help you determine how you will use it. For instance, if you have small children, you may want to review a story several times, extending the activity that goes with it for more than one day. Or you may want to switch activities from one day to another, depending on your family's schedule or the type of activity. Don't think that you need to try everything the first time you use this book. There are enough ideas here to last for several seasons.

As you plan, keep in mind these things:
- Choose a regular time and place to meet each day.
- Involve your children in the preparation for each day's activity.
- Read through all directions carefully before you begin. Necessary supplies are listed at the beginning of each activity. Most supplies are readily available and you may already have them on hand.
- When reading the folk stories and legends with your children, explain that these stories are not the same as Bible stories. Young children need help in understanding that there is a difference between Bible truths and legends people create.
- Take turns reading each day's Bible passage. Then spend time reflecting on the text. By establishing the habit of family Bible reading and discussion, your children will come to look forward to hearing God's Word. In the Lenten section, weekly scripture verses have been assigned. For the rest of the book, appropriate verses have been assigned to each day. Commit the verses to memory, or include them in a moment of family prayer.

However you use this book, it is hoped that it will bring deeper meaning to your family's observances of the days before and after Easter!

3

LENT

History and traditions

The word *Lent* comes from the Anglo-Saxon word that means "spring" or "springtime." Taken literally, the word means that this is the time of the year when the days *lengthen.* This season of the church year is a time of preparation, reflection, growth, and change.

As God's people take the time to learn more about God and their relationship to God and to others, the season before Easter can be seen as the springtime of the soul—a time of growth in faith and a time to nurture the faith that is already theirs.

The Christian faith centers around the death and resurrection of Jesus Christ. We need to see this event from both sides—before and after—because each side of the story is incomplete without the other.

The season of Lent began in the early church as a time for preparing new converts for Baptism on Easter. By the middle of the fourth century, a 40-day preparation period had been established. During that time, candidates for Baptism fasted and heard lectures from early church leaders. Later, the season of Lent became a time for all Christians to prepare for Easter. It remains a 40-day long period, not counting Sundays. Historically the Lenten fasts were lessened on Sundays, thus not included in the days of Lent. All Sundays are considered "little Easters," celebrating the resurrection.

The season of Lent begins for many people on Shrove Tuesday, but it officially begins on Ash Wednesday and continues until Easter morning.

By the year A.D. 400 the early Christian church had established this period of 40 days. It became a time of self-discipline and harsh self-examination, and during the Middle Ages, the season of Lent was so strict that people dreaded its coming.

Through time, the harsh demands and expectations have been softened and relaxed. People today look to Lent as a time of growth and change. They often include fasting or restriction of some of their favorite foods or drinks during the 40 days of Lent. Some people spend more time in prayer and meditation while others give up habits they think are unnecessary. Still others search to discover how they can share God's love with others in the world in meaningful ways.

Purple is the color associated with the season of Lent and is used in churches that observe liturgical traditions. Purple is a solemn color, reminiscent of royalty and repentance. It reflects the serious and somber nature of this time in the life of the church.

Counting the days

It is common practice for people to count the days of Advent in anticipation of Christmas Day. It is just as significant to mark the days of Lent, beginning with Ash Wednesday and leading to the most celebrated of festivals, Easter Sunday.

One way to do this is with a devotional book written specifically for this season. Many are available for adult use, but children often need a visual reminder of the days to help them see the big picture. Several Lenten calendar suggestions are included here for your family to make, adapt, and use. Choose one of these ideas and make it your family's own special way of counting the days until Easter.

Christmas tree cross

How symbolic to take the trunk from your natural Christmas tree and use it during your Lenten family time! Of course, this will take some pre-planning to cut and save the trunk until Lent begins, and you may want to substitute other wood in place of the tree trunk, or save this idea for another year.

To make a Christmas tree cross, trim away the tree branches and cut two pieces for the cross, one approximately 15″ long and the other 13″ long. You may adjust the size accordingly. Notch the longer piece about one-third of the way from one end and notch the shorter piece in the middle, so that the pieces will fit snugly together. Glue in place. You may want to use two small nails to fasten the wood securely.

Choose seven purple candles—one for each week of Lent—and drill a hole for each in the tree cross as shown. Because this is such a long season, you will want to buy several extra candles to replace those burned most. Purchase seven white candles for use on Easter morning.

Each day, during your family time, light one of the candles as you read the Bible text or finish with prayer. Remember never to leave burning candles unattended.

Crown of thorns wreath

Make a crown of thorns wreath to use as a way of counting the days of Lent. Grapevine wreaths can be purchased in most craft stores, or you can make one with wild honeysuckle or other vines you may have growing in your own yard. If you make your own wreath base, you may or may not choose to have one that has actual thorns.

Insert and wire seven purple candles to the wreath, setting one large white candle in the center. To use this wreath, light one candle for the first week of Lent, two candles for the second week, and so on. Because of the length of this season, you may have to replace some of the candles as you near Holy Week. During that week, begin with all of the candles lit, then extinguish one each day so that you end on the Saturday before Easter with no candles lit. If you celebrate the Easter Vigil (see p. 55) and stay up past midnight, light the large white candle to represent Christ's resurrection at that time. Otherwise, light the white candle on Easter morning in celebration of the resurrection.

Paper chains

Even young children can participate in making paper chains. Cut 40 2″ wide strips of purple paper—one for each day in Lent—and a white strip for Easter. Since Sundays are not included in the 40 days of Lent, to represent each Sunday, cut seven strips of another color.

Then have everyone write on the strips things they might do to share their faith during this time of preparation. For example, invite a friend to church or help an elderly neighbor walk the dog. As a family, you might decide to help out at a local food pantry or soup kitchen. Help children who are too young to write to either draw a simple picture of what they will do or write it for them. Make Sundays a time of doing something fun together as a family. Sundays could include special family worship and praise activities.

Staple or tape the chain links together: six purple links, then one of another color to represent Sunday, and so on, ending with the one white chain link representing Easter Day. Hang the chain in a special place and remove one link each day to count the days of Lent, doing what is written on the strips and remembering other ways you can share your faith.

Shrove Tuesday
(The day before Lent begins)

"A man can do nothing better than to eat and drink and find satisfaction in his work. This too, I see, is from the hand of God, for without him, who can eat or find enjoyment?" Ecclesiastes 2:24-25

The celebration before the fast

Lent is a time of self-discipline and denial. Throughout the 40 days of Lent, people are called to fasting and prayer. But the week preceding Lent has become a time of merrymaking, culminating on Shrove Tuesday, or Fat Tuesday, the day before Lent begins.

The name Shrove Tuesday comes from the custom of ringing the "shriving bell" to summon the people to church to be "shriven," that is, to confess their sins at the beginning of Lent. At that time, certain foods were given up for the duration of Lent. Those foods included eggs, milk, meat, and rich buttery dishes. On Shrove Tuesday, families ate up all the rich foods left in their pantries. One way they used up the eggs, milk, and fats in the house was to add flour to make special pancakes. In England, the popularity of pancakes caused Shrove Tuesday to be called Pancake Day, and festivities surrounded the eating of pancakes, including pancake races.

Still another name for Shrove Tuesday is *Mardi Gras* or *Carnival*. Mardi Gras is celebrated with dancing, feasting, parades, and merrymaking in many cities in Spain, France, Italy, and Portugal. Two of the most famous celebrations take place in Rio De Janeiro, Brazil, and in New Orleans, Louisiana, in the United States. Celebrations move through the streets of these cities until midnight on Shrove Tuesday when Ash Wednesday comes and Lent begins.

A celebration of your own

Make your own Shrove Tuesday celebration Pancake Day this year. Following are some extra-special pancake recipes.

Pancake shapes. Pour your pancake batter into a squeeze bottle and squeeze out special shaped cakes or write names with the batter.

Pigs 'n blankets. Spread pancakes with butter or margarine, then roll them around cooked sausages. Pour on your favorite syrup and serve.

Cherry toppers. Spread sour cream or whipped cream topping over the pancakes and top with cherry pie filling.

Fruity syrup. Mix together one 3-ounce package of fruit flavored gelatin, ½ cup sugar, 2 teaspoons corn starch, and 1 cup water. Boil slowly until mixture thickens. Pour on your pancakes and enjoy!

Puffy oven pancakes. Preheat oven to 425°. Melt 2 tablespoons butter or margarine in bottom of pie pan in the oven, while mixing the pancake batter. For batter, combine 1 egg, ¼ cup flour, and ¼ cup milk (batter will be lumpy). When the butter is sizzling, pour batter into pie pan and sprinkle with nutmeg. Bake for about 15 minutes, or until pancake is puffy and golden colored. Remove from oven and serve immediately with powdered sugar and jam or syrup on top. You have to move quickly before the pancake falls!

Ash Wednesday (Day 1)

"Therefore, since we are surrounded by such a great cloud of witnesses, let us throw off everything that hinders and the sin that so easily entangles, and let us run with perseverance the race marked out for us."   Hebrews 12:1

A visible sign of repentance

Ash Wednesday is the first day in the season of Lent. It is a day of fasting and prayer and a time when we can publicly confess the sin that entangles us.

The ashes of this first day in Lent are a symbol that has been derived from several ancient customs. In the Old Testament, people put on sackcloth and ashes when they were in mourning. As far back as the third century, ashes were worn on the body as a visible sign of sin and a public request for forgiveness. Ashes were also used sometimes as a cleanser when soap was not available. And, in times past, farmers would burn off their fields in the spring, turning dried stubble to ash before new planting began. Thus, ashes become a symbol of repentance *and* renewal.

Today, many churches hold special services where the palms from the previous Palm Sunday are burned, then mixed with oil and used to mark the sign of the cross on the forehead of those attending. The ashen cross is a visible reminder of our need for repentance and forgiveness.

Soap cross

Supplies: Bar of soft hand soap (such as Ivory); table knife or plastic knife; pencil.

The ashen cross of Ash Wednesday reminds us of our need for repentance and forgiveness. Carve a cross from soap to remind one another of how Jesus washed away our sins on the cross.

Draw a cross shape on the bar of soap, then carefully carve away the excess soap. A dull knife should work fine on soft soap. (Save the soap chips in a bottle and add a little water to them to make liquid hand soap.)

As you wash with the soap cross, remember to thank God for forgiving us.

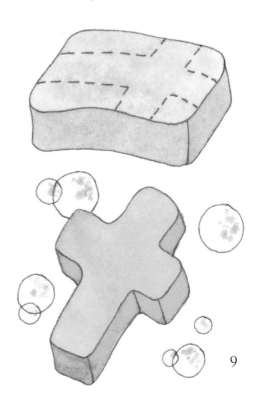

9

Day 2

"Therefore, since we are surrounded by such a great cloud of witnesses, let us throw off everything that hinders and the sin that so easily entangles, and let us run with perseverance the race marked out for us."　　　*Hebrews 12:1*

Fasting and prayer

After Jesus was baptized by John at the Jordan River, he went off into the wilderness for forty days. During that time, Jesus went without food and water, and he was tempted by the devil. When the devil suggested that Jesus turn stones into bread, Jesus replied, "Man does not live on bread alone, but on every word that comes from the mouth of God" (Matt. 4:4).

Fasting is mentioned quite frequently in the Bible. Abstaining from food or drink was usually done as a sign of mourning for sins. But fasting involves more than not eating. Prayer always should go along with fasting. Jesus taught that prayer and fasting were not to be public spectacles (Matt. 6:5-18). When we fast and pray, we turn to God alone.

During Lent we are encouraged to reflect on our relationship with God. One way we can do that is through fasting and prayer. Our fasts do not need to be long; occasionally going without a meal and spending that time meditating on God's Word can help one experience fasting.

Meatless meal

As an alternative to fasting, consider reducing your family's meat consumption at some meals. Try this recipe for a nutritious and tasty alternative for meat in a meal.

Refrito spread

Ingredients:
1½ cups cooked, drained beans
　　(pinto, kidney, or black), mashed
1 onion, chopped
1 tablespoon oil
¼ cup green pepper, chopped
½ cup cheddar cheese, grated
seasonings to taste—garlic, cumin,
　　chili powder

Saute onion and green pepper in oil until tender. Add mashed beans, and seasoning to taste. Cook on low heat until heated through. Let cool slightly. Stir in cheese. Spread on tortillas or other bread.

Day 3

"Therefore, since we are surrounded by such a great cloud of witnesses, let us throw off everything that hinders and the sin that so easily entangles, and let us run with perseverance the race marked out for us." Hebrews 12:1

The widow's offering

As Jesus and his disciples sat in the temple, they watched people come to offer their gifts to God. One woman in particular caught Jesus' eye.

This woman, a poor widow, came and put two small coins into the treasury. While others gave only some of their wealth—from their abundance—this woman gave everything that she had.

During Lent, we take time to think about the gifts we offer to God and the spirit in which we give them. Do we give only some of what we have, or do we give everything that we have?

Coin counter

Some people purchase a special coin folder to save money during Lent—perhaps money they would have spent on a luxury item. Some people choose to give up something and then contribute to their church the money they would have spent.

Make your own family coin counter to save money for a special family offering, perhaps to share with a local or national agency that provides food or shelter for the homeless.

Your coin counter may be as simple as a can with a plastic lid that you have decorated and cut a slit in the lid. Another coin counter could be made from a piece of poster board with small envelopes glued to it to make a "pocket chart." Each pocket could be labeled with the date and possibly the particular concern that the money will be given for. You may also want to print on the envelope a word of something you as a family can be thankful for as a focus for prayer or meditation. At the end of the season of Lent, count the money together as a family and give it to the appropriate charities.

Day 4

"Therefore, since we are surrounded by such a great cloud of witnesses, let us throw off everything that hinders and the sin that so easily entangles, and let us run with perseverance the race marked out for us."   *Hebrews 12:1*

Giving up everything to follow Jesus

One day early in his ministry, Jesus was walking by the sea of Galilee. There he saw two brothers fishing offshore. He called out to them, "Come! Follow me and I will teach you to catch people!" Immediately the fishermen left their boats to follow Jesus.

My family is a fishing family. I grew up in a fishing town where the smell of fish is part of everyday life. I know that boats and nets and fishing gear are expensive, not only in monetary value, but in the time and energy invested in keeping them in good repair and working order. These fishermen left their equipment—their livelihood—to follow someone they knew little about.

The first people that Jesus called to follow him were not scholars or religious leaders. They were ordinary people. They had no special qualifications; yet Jesus chose them. Even though we also are ordinary people, we also are called to follow Jesus. We have been chosen to leave behind the trappings of the world and carry the message of Jesus, sharing the good news with the people we meet every day.

Tissue paper fish symbols

Supplies: Brightly colored tissue paper; scissors; white glue; nylon monofilament thread; felt-tip pens.

The fish was a symbol used by some of the earliest Christians. Make your own fish symbols to tell the world that you also follow Jesus.

Lay two sheets of tissue paper together and cut a fish shape. Run a thin line of glue along the edge of one fish shape, leaving a portion of the tail unglued. Gently place the other piece on top.

When the glue is dry, use a felt-tip pen to add features to the fish such as fin lines, eyes, and gills. Gently stuff the fish shape with crumpled tissue paper and glue the tail end shut. Poke a small hole at the top and tie a length of nylon monofilament thread to hang the fish.

Day 5

"May my prayer be set before you like incense; may the lifting up of my hands be like the evening sacrifice." *Psalm 141:2*

The story of the "little arms"

It was about the year A.D. 672 in a monastery in the German Alps. Every day Brother John measured, mixed, rolled, kneaded, and baked hearty breads, cookies, and cakes for the people of the village to buy. He worked in the bakery kitchen with Brother Boniface, who allowed him to create special treats for the children he loved.

"Are these the sacks of flour for the Lenten bread?" Brother Boniface asked Brother John one morning. "Next Tuesday is Shrove Tuesday and we will need to begin baking early that morning if we are to make enough bread for the entire village."

"I know," Brother John replied. "After the shriving bell rings at midnight, Lent begins. Then we will eat less and pray more," he added as he crossed his arms and put his hands on his shoulders in prayer as he had learned to do. "And then, Brother Boniface, it will be time for little arms!"

"What are little arms?" Brother Boniface asked in a puzzled voice. "I haven't heard of them before."

"In my country of Italy," Brother John told him, "we make our bread into the shape of little arms. We mix the flour and water and then twist the dough into the shape of praying arms to remind us that Lent is a special time to pray."

"That is a wonderful type of Lenten bread!" Brother Boniface said. "Will you teach me to make these little arms?"

And so Brother John taught Brother Boniface to make little arms. When the little arms were ready to come out of the oven, Brother Boniface smiled and laughed.

"In our language," he said, "we call your 'little arms' *pretzels.*"

And so it happened that pretzels became part of our Lenten tradition, even to this day.

You may be used to thinking of pretzels as heart shaped, but turn one upside down to see the shape of the crossed arms.

Soft pretzels

Ingredients:
1 package of dry yeast
1½ cups warm water
1 tablespoon sugar
4 cups flour
1 beaten egg
coarse salt

Dissolve the yeast in water. Then add the sugar and salt. Blend in the flour and turn the dough onto a lightly floured board. Knead until smooth. Cut off slices of the dough and roll them into ropes. Twist the ropes into pretzel shapes and arrange them on a cookie sheet lined with greased brown paper. Brush the pretzels with the egg and sprinkle coarse salt on them. Bake in a 425° oven for 12-15 minutes or until golden brown.

Day 6

"May my prayer be set before you like incense; may the lifting up of my hands be like the evening sacrifice."   *Psalm 141:2*

The prayer Jesus taught

The disciples had much to learn from Jesus. They questioned him about the kingdom of God, about forgiveness, and about prayer. Their questions are often our questions—even today. Jesus taught the disciples about prayer through words, as well as through his own life of prayer. Take time during Lent to follow Jesus' example of prayer in your own life, perhaps finding your own "lonely" place and meditating on one phrase of the Lord's Prayer each day. (See Matt. 6:9-15.)

Pray with movement

Our Father, who art in heaven,
hallowed be thy name,
(Raise hands overhead, then put palms together.)

thy kingdom come, thy will be done,
on earth as it is in heaven.
(Slowly lower hands in a circular motion, ending
with hands in front of you.)

Give us this day our daily bread;
(Turn palms up in a receiving gesture.)

and forgive us our trespasses,
(Bow head with hands at sides.)

as we forgive those who trespass against us;
(Lift arms and join hands with others.)

and lead us not into temptation,
(Fold arms across chest.)

but deliver us from evil.
(Arms straight down with palms together.)

For thine is the kingdom, and the power,
and the glory, forever and ever. Amen
(Raise hands into the praying position and bow head.)

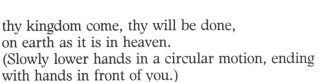

Day 7

"May my prayer be set before you like incense; may the lifting up of my hands be like the evening sacrifice."   Psalm 141:2

The legend of the Phoenix

An ancient legend tells about the Phoenix, a majestic and beautiful bird with feathers and plumes of all colors. This bird lived in the land of Arabia.

Now only one Phoenix was allowed to live on the earth at a time, and each bird lived for about 500 years. When the time was near for this magical bird to die, it would build a nest of spices and herbs such as frankincense and myrrh. Then the great Phoenix would set the nest on fire and sit within its flames to die. As the embers of the fire died down, out of the ashes would rise a new Phoenix. For some Christians in the early church, this story of the Phoenix became a symbol of the resurrection of Jesus who died and then rose again to life.

Make your own incense

In the Bible, incense is symbolic of prayers rising to heaven. (See Ps. 141:2 and Rev. 8:3-5.) A simple way to create your own incense is to throw the stems of small bundles of herbs into the fireplace. Lavender stems stripped of the leaves and inserted into a flowerpot filled with sand can be lit on the tips to fill the air with their perfume. Or, you can mix together this recipe:

2 tablespoons dried ground sage
2 tablespoons dried and ground eucalyptus leaves
2 tablespoons dried and ground redwood or cedar needles
2 tablespoons dried and ground pine needles
1½ tablespoons dried balsam sap grains
pinch of salt

Mix the ingredients together thoroughly and burn in a fireplace or incense burner.

Day 8

"May my prayer be set before you like incense; may the lifting up of my hands be like the evening sacrifice."   *Psalm 141:2*

World Day of Prayer

A common theme for the Lenten season is prayer. While you may decide to spend more time in private prayer during Lent, you may also wish to join with others in a time of corporate conversation with God.

World Day of Prayer is observed on the first Friday in Lent. On that day, Christians throughout the world gather in churches to pray together. The prayer services usually focus on mutual understanding between the peoples of the world and on world peace.

Many communities hold World Day of Prayer services. Often several churches come together for a joint service. Your family may wish to attend a prayer service in your community as a special Lenten observance this year.

Seven continents

Tack a large world map to a wall in a central place in your home or place a globe in the center of your kitchen table. Talk with your family about the different countries of the world, noting the differences in topographical and geographical features. Point out the seven continents of the world (North and South America, Europe, Asia, Africa, Australia, and Antarctica), and spend time researching and discussing what the lives of the people on each continent are like.

After you have done this background work, include the people and the government leaders of the countries of one continent per day in your family time of prayer.

17

Day 9

"May my prayer be set before you like incense; may the lifting up of my hands be like the evening sacrifice."   *Psalm 141:2*

The story of the praying hands

More than 500 years ago a baby boy was born to a poor family in Nuremberg, Germany. The father of the child was a goldsmith and he intended his son to follow him in the trade. But young Albrecht Dürer had other ideas. He wanted to be an artist.

At the age of thirteen, he showed his father a drawing that he had done. His father was astounded by the boy's artistic talent. He decided that Albrecht's talent would be wasted as a goldsmith, and so the boy was apprenticed to the master artist of Nuremberg.

Albrecht Dürer grew to be a renowned artist. His etchings, woodcuts, engravings, and paintings are prized as great works of art today. But Dürer was more than an artist. He was a devout Christian whose works were done to the glory of God. One of his most famous works today is a small study he did while working on "The Heller Altar-Piece." We know it as "The Praying Hands."

A story is told that a friend went to work in the fields to help Dürer pay for his art education. In return, once Dürer was finished with school, he would work to pay for his friend's education. But the friend toiled so hard that his hands were made stiff, and when the time came for him to begin his studies, he was not able to. Some say that it was the hands of this sacrificing friend that Dürer used as a model for his famous work.

Five-finger prayers

Use your fingers as prayer reminders. The thumb can remind us to pray for friends and family. The index finger is a reminder to pray for people who point us to God (pastors, teachers, parents). The middle finger is the tallest, so it can remind us to pray for the people who are leaders in our cities, states, and countries. The ring finger is the weakest finger and can remind us to pray for those people who are less fortunate than we are. Finally, the littlest finger can be a reminder to pray for ourselves.

Day 10

"May my prayer be set before you like incense; may the lifting up of my hands be like the evening sacrifice."   *Psalm 141:2*

What you have in your hand

Have you ever noticed that sometimes the things we have right in our hands are too close for us to see? We may take for granted what we have. We often overlook the everyday blessings around us, and forget to include these blessings in our prayers of thanks. During Lent and throughout the year, make an intentional effort to notice the blessings in your life and daily offer prayers of thanksgiving to God for things large and small.

"Good Fortune" cookies

Count your blessings with these special fortune cookies! Have each family member write on a small slip of paper some blessing they are thankful for. Then make the following cookies and insert the blessings slips. After a family meal, break open the cookies and read the blessings aloud. Offer a prayer of thanks for all the blessings God has given you. And remember to pray for those people who are less fortunate than you are.

Ingredients:
¼ cup sifted cake flour
2 tablespoons sugar
1 tablespoon cornstarch
Dash salt
2 tablespoons oil
1 egg white
1 tablespoon water

Stir together the dry ingredients. Add oil and egg white and stir until smooth. Add water and mix thoroughly. Lightly grease a skillet or griddle. Pour 1 tablespoon of the batter into the skillet and spread into a 3½" circle, using the back of a spoon. Cook over low heat until lightly brown (about 4 minutes). Flip over and cook for one minute more.

Remove the cookie from the pan and place on a clean potholder. Put a blessings slip in the center of the circle and fold the cookie in half over it. Fold the cookie in half again by placing it over the edge of a bowl. Cool cookies in a muffin tin to hold their shape. Makes 8 cookies.

Day 11

"And God said, 'This is a sign of the covenant I am making between me and you and every living creature with you, a covenant for all generations to come.'" — Genesis 9:12

Markers of our faith

In the Old Testament, God placed a visible sign in the sky to remind Noah and his family of the promise never again to destroy the earth with a flood. The rainbow was a symbol of God's covenant with the people. Whenever a rainbow appears in the sky, we also can remember God's promise, and know that promise is sure.

Signs and symbols are reminders for us. As Christians, we use a variety of symbols to reflect the faith we share in Christ Jesus. The symbols on pages 21-22 are ones associated with Lent and Easter. Talk about what the different symbols represent. What other symbols are meaningful to you?

New life tree

Supplies: a tree branch; coffee can or flowerpot; gravel or plaster of Paris; crayons; vegetable peeler or grater; waxed paper; newspaper; scissors; pencil; paper punch; yarn; iron.

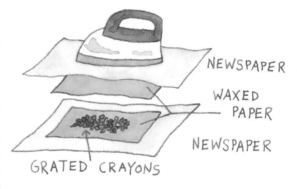

NEWSPAPER

WAXED PAPER

NEWSPAPER

GRATED CRAYONS

If you and your family plan to have an Easter egg tree (see p. 57), you might want to make a tree of Lenten symbols to use for now, removing these symbol designs and replacing them with Easter eggs or Easter symbols on Easter Sunday.

Anchor the tree branch in the can or pot filled with gravel or plaster of Paris. Choose some of the symbol designs from pages 21-22 to make to hang from the branch. Place waxed paper over the symbols you choose and trace around the outlines to make patterns. Cut out the patterns.

For each symbol, place a piece of waxed paper on newspaper and grate assorted colors of crayons over it. Lay another piece of waxed paper on top and cover with a layer of newspaper. Press with a warm iron until the wax seeps through the newspaper. Carefully peel the newspaper away from the waxed paper. Place the symbol pattern on top of the now-colored wax paper and trace around it. Cut out the symbol and punch a hole at the top. String a length of yarn through the hole to make a hanger. (See Day 12 for another symbol-making idea.)

20

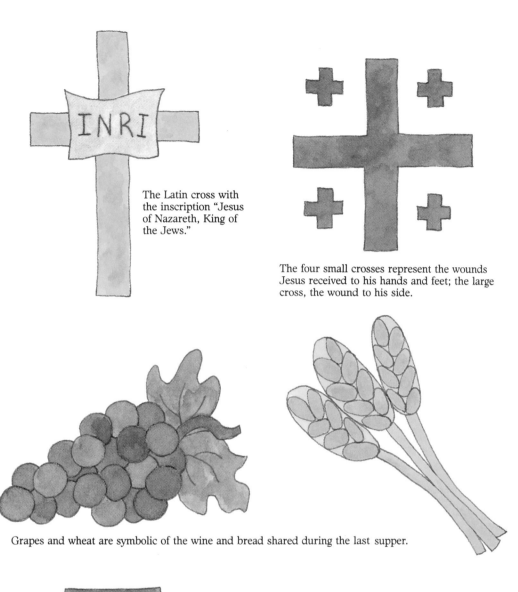

The Latin cross with the inscription "Jesus of Nazareth, King of the Jews."

The four small crosses represent the wounds Jesus received to his hands and feet; the large cross, the wound to his side.

Grapes and wheat are symbolic of the wine and bread shared during the last supper.

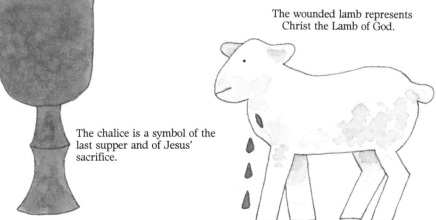

The wounded lamb represents Christ the Lamb of God.

The chalice is a symbol of the last supper and of Jesus' sacrifice.

The palm branch reminds us of Jesus' entry into Jerusalem.

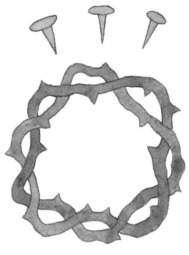

The crown of thorns and three nails are symbols of the crucifixion.

A bag of coins reminds us of the 30 pieces of silver for which Judas betrayed Jesus.

The rooster recalls Peter's denial of Jesus.

The butterfly is a symbol of the resurrection.

Day 12

"And God said, 'This is a sign of the covenant I am making between me and you and every living creature with you, a covenant for all generations to come.'"   *Genesis 9:12*

The symbols of Lent

Although most of the symbols of the Christian faith are used and recognized throughout the year, several are particularly significant during the season of Lent. These include: palm branches to represent when Jesus entered Jerusalem, grapes and wheat as symbols of the Last Supper, the crown of thorns with three nails, the Latin cross with the inscription "Jesus of Nazareth, King of the Jews," and a wounded lamb.

Foil "stained-glass" symbols

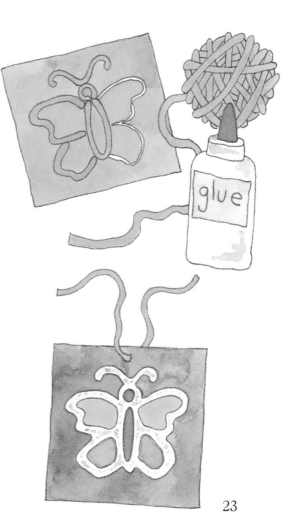

Supplies: Aluminum foil; permanent felt-tip markers; string or yarn; white glue; poster board or thin cardboard cut into 3″ squares; paper punch; tape.

Use this technique to make more symbols to add to your "new life" tree (see p. 20).

Sketch one of the symbols from pages 21-22 onto a square of poster board, then trace over with a thin line of glue. Press a length of string or yarn onto the glue and let dry. When the glue is thoroughly dry, lay a piece of foil *larger than the poster board* over the design, and carefully run your finger on either side of the string to cover the poster board with the foil and make the string a raised design. Fold the extra foil to the back, and tape down if necessary. Use permanent felt-tip pens to color in the design. Punch a hole in the top, add a loop of string, and hang from the tree.

Day 13

"And God said, 'This is a sign of the covenant I am making between me and you and every living creature with you, a covenant for all generations to come.'"   Genesis 9:12

The story of the first hot cross buns

Long ago in England, a monk saw poor families living in their tents on the streets of his town.

"It is not right," the monk thought to himself, "that with Easter only two days away these families should go hungry."

Because this monk had once been a baker, he decided to make many buns with spices and raisins inside. After the spicy buns came out of the oven, he decorated the tops with a white frosting cross. Then he took the buns, while they were still warm, and shared them with the families he had seen.

There was one young boy who was so proud that he would not even take one bun. "Give me a basketful of buns to sell," he said. "I do not want to take your charity."

So the monk did. And on that Easter morning, the young boy proudly carried his basket of buns from house to house, singing this song that you may know:

Hot cross buns! Hot cross buns!
One a penny, two a penny. Hot cross buns!
If you have no daughters, give them to your sons.
One a penny, two a penny. Hot cross buns!

Before the church service began that Easter morning, the young boy had sold all of the buns. And he put the money into the offering box at church as he went to celebrate the joy of the risen Christ.

Hot cross buns

Make your own version of hot cross buns using your own bread or roll recipe, or by purchasing a loaf of frozen bread dough and shaping it into buns. Add a cross of white sugar frosting to the tops of the buns. You might even want to share a basketful with your neighbors, or with a family that you would like to invite to visit your church.

FOR THE COOPERS

Day 14

"And God said, 'This is a sign of the covenant I am making between me and you and every living creature with you, a covenant for all generations to come.'"
Genesis 9:12

The donkey's legend

It is said that at the time Jesus lived, there was a small donkey that lived near Jerusalem with his master. Now this donkey didn't seem to be able to do anything right, and his master decided he couldn't continue to feed the donkey that wouldn't work. When he decided to kill the donkey, his children begged him to sell it instead.

"How can I sell a donkey that will not work?" the man asked the children.

So his son suggested, "Father, tie this donkey to a tree on the road into the town. Let everyone know that whoever wants it may take it for nothing."

And the next morning that is just what the farmer did.

Very soon after that, two men approached and asked to take the donkey. But the farmer warned them, "This donkey will do no work!"

"That is not our concern," the men said. "The Lord has need of it." So even though the farmer could not imagine what the Lord would do with a worthless donkey, he gave it to the two men.

The two men took the donkey to Jesus, who was waiting for it. Jesus was pleased at the sight of the little donkey, and he patted it reassuringly. "You will be safe now, my little one," he said as he climbed on the donkey's back.

And so it was that on the day we now call Palm Sunday, Jesus rode into the town of Jerusalem on the back of the little donkey. And there was a great crowd that followed them shouting "Hosanna! Hosanna! Blessed be the one who comes in the name of the Lord!"

Even today, if you look at the back of the little Castilian donkey, you will notice that a dark patch of hair goes down its back, and then crosses at its shoulders. Ever since Jesus rode into Jerusalem on the back of the little donkey, the donkey has worn a cross on its back.

A cross of nails

Supplies: One 2" nail and one 1½" nail for the simple cross, two 2" nails for the variation; thin picture-hanging wire; purple or black yarn or cording; hammer; pliers (optional).

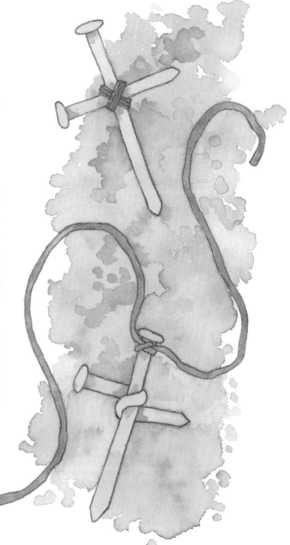

Make a cross of nails to wear as a reminder of how much Jesus loves you.

Blunt the ends of the nails by hammering the sharp end slightly.

To make a simple nail cross, lay the 1½" nail across the 2" nail, about one-third of the distance from the nail-head. Bind the nails together by tightly wrapping the wire around the two nails, using a criss-cross technique as shown. Cover the wire by wrapping in the same manner using the yarn or cord.

For a variation, use the pliers to bend one of the 2" nails around the other, attaching in place inside the twist as shown. Glue, if necessary. Attach a length of yarn or cording to wear the cross around your neck.

Day 15

"And God said, 'This is a sign of the covenant I am making between me and you and every living creature with you, a covenant for all generations to come.'"
Genesis 9:12

The symbol of the butterfly

Of all of the symbols Christians use to represent new life, the butterfly is definitely one of the most well known. The caterpillar in its chrysalis represents Christ in the tomb for three days. Then, as the emerging butterfly appears, we are reminded of Jesus' resurrection and the new life that comes through it.

A caterpillar cage

Supplies: Two empty 7½ ounce cans with the top lids removed (tuna or cat food cans work well); file; pencil; hammer; nail; small piece of wood; fine screen, 7″ x 2″; stapler; about 16″ of string or yarn; leaves and tree branches; caterpillar.

Thoroughly wash the cans. File down any sharp edges. Mark a dot in the center of the inside bottom of each can, then place the can on the piece of wood and hammer the nail through the mark to make a hole. Remove the nail.

Form the screen into a 7″ high cylinder that will fit snugly inside the two cans as shown. Staple the screen along the side where it overlaps.

Tie a knot in one end of a piece of string, and thread it up through the hole in the bottom can, through the screen cylinder and through the hole in the top can. Tie a loop at the top for hanging. Be sure to leave an inch or two of slack to slide the top can up to put fresh leaves in the cage.

Place a caterpillar or two, as well as the leaves and twigs that were near the caterpillar, in the cage. (Replace the leaves frequently.) Be patient and watch to see if the caterpillar begins the metamorphosis process, forming a cocoon and eventually turns into a butterfly.

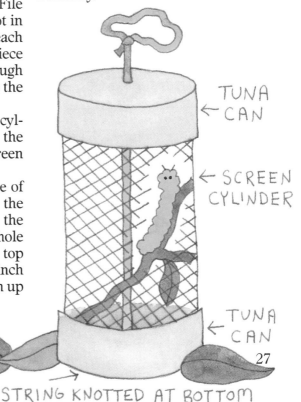

TUNA ← CAN

← SCREEN CYLINDER

TUNA ← CAN

27

STRING KNOTTED AT BOTTOM

Day 16

"And God said, 'This is a sign of the covenant I am making between me and you and every living creature with you, a covenant for all generations to come.' "
Genesis 9:12

The legend of the dogwood

Many years ago, there was a dogwood tree growing on the hill outside of the city of Jerusalem. At that time the dogwood tree was one of the tallest and mightiest of the trees; as strong as an oak tree. And this particular tree was the tallest of all the dogwoods and very proud of it too.

To everyone who passed by, this dogwood would brag, "I know that something wonderful will happen to me. Perhaps I'll become the mast that holds the sails on a great sailing ship, or the beam that supports a house or temple."

As time passed and the tree continued to grow, it could only wonder as to what it would become. One day it happened. The proud dogwood tree was cut down. But the tree did not become a mast or even a beam. Instead it became the cross on which Jesus was nailed for the crucifixion. The tree was horrified and it groaned in agony as the two pieces of its trunk were nailed into the shape of the cross.

Now as Jesus carried the cross to Calvary, he took pity on the tree. "You will never be used in this way again," he said. "From this day, your shape will be changed, just as the world will change after my death. You will become a slender tree of great beauty that sways gently in the breeze. And instead of acorns, you will bear white flowers in the shape of the cross. In the center of the flowers there will be a crown of thorns, a reminder forever that I spent my last hours with you. And each petal will carry red stains to show how you have suffered with me."

Have you seen the flowers of the dogwood tree? They appear just as the legend says.

Signs of spring

After long months of winter, we look eagerly for signs of spring. In the midst of Lent, it is good to realize that spring, with its promise of new life, will soon be here. Try bringing a bit of spring indoors to brighten your winter hearts!

If you have a pussy willow or forsythia bush in your yard, cut some branches. Bringing them into the warmth of your house can force them into bloom.

Cut the branches on a slant and set them in a container of warm water. Set the container in a cool place, like a basement, until the branches begin to leaf out. Soon, the water and the warmth will cause them to bloom—a sure sign of the spring to come!

Day 17

"The King will reply, 'I tell you the truth, whatever you did for one of the least of these brothers of mine, you did for me.'" Matthew 25:40

Who are your neighbors?

Our lives seem to be so full with appointments, job responsibilities, and obligations, that it is easy to neglect or even not notice the people in the world around us. Many of us don't even know our neighbors well enough to call them by name.

In Luke 10:25-37, Jesus answers a question about who is our neighbor by telling a parable about a man in trouble. If Jesus were to tell the story of the good Samaritan today, do you suppose the people who passed by would hesitate to help not because of their distaste for the man, but rather because they did not even take the time to *see* him?

Take the time today to examine your own busy life. Make a conscious effort to notice and respond to those who are hurting and in need around you, whether they are your physical neighbors or people who live far away. What better way to share the good news of the faith-filled life you have as a member of God's family!

In service

How can your family be of service to others? If your church contributes to a local agency such as a food or clothing bank, why not collect items to add to the effort? Better yet, volunteer as a family to spend time working at the facility, sharing your love in tangible ways.

If you are not aware of a program of sharing in your community, brainstorm with your family and friends to find a need and fill it. Maybe a care facility needs volunteers to visit with residents or needs ramps built or repaired. Perhaps a child care facility needs sand or play chips delivered and spread for the playground. Could you begin a blanket drive or help a local school set up backpacks for use by children if they are stranded at school during an emergency caused by weather or natural disaster? With a little thoughtful planning and time, you and your family can make a difference as "good Samaritans" of today!

Day 18

"The King will reply, 'I tell you the truth, whatever you did for one of the least of these brothers of mine, you did for me.'"   *Matthew 25:40*

Love in action

When God sent Jesus to earth, it was the greatest gift God could have given us. Without the love and sacrifice of Jesus on the cross, we would not know the joy of the resurrection or the sure and certain hope of eternal life.

We may not always be sure what we can give God in return. But we can show our love for God by our gifts of love and service. Through the many different ways that we share the good news of the gospel with the people in our world, God knows of our love.

Sharing our gifts

Does your family have a special way of sharing out of your abundance? Here is a snack that might be fun to make and share with people you know. Or you might wish to share it with some people whom you'd like to know better, such as the elderly couple down the block or the single parent across the street or the new tenants who just moved in upstairs. Enjoy!

Krispy mix

Ingredients:
4 cups of assorted krispy cereal squares
⅓ cup melted butter or margarine
1½ cup pretzels
½ cup assorted dry roasted nuts
½ cup raisins or date pieces
seasonings to taste, such as garlic powder

Spread the cereal squares onto a baking sheet and cover with the melted butter or margarine. Sprinkle on seasoning, if you wish. Bake at 350° for 15 minutes, stirring often. Remove from the oven and add the remaining ingredients, mixing well.

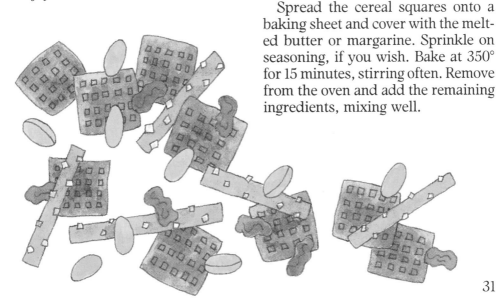

Day 19

"The King will reply, 'I tell you the truth, whatever you did for one of the least of these brothers of mine, you did for me.'"   *Matthew 25:40*

The story of Zacchaeus

In Luke 19:1-10 is recorded the story of Zacchaeus, the tax collector. The story of Zacchaeus is a favorite of children, possibly because they can identify with the man who had to climb a tree in order to see Jesus, because he couldn't see over the heads of the crowd. Children often have the disadvantage of not being able to see. It can make them feel insignificant.

Perhaps Zacchaeus felt insignificant too. But Jesus changed all that. He saw the man in the tree and called for him to come down. Even more, he went to the man's house to stay for the day! Jesus' loving act changed Zacchaeus' life. Our loving acts can change the lives of others. We can make people feel significant. We can recognize that everyone has gifts to offer— even little children.

A family giving tree

Many families are aware of their "family tree"—a listing of their ancestors and present relatives. Why not make a family *giving* tree along these lines?

Draw a tree shape on a large sheet of paper, adding the names of current family members to the branches. As a family, talk about the kinds of gifts you give to one another and notice how many of these gifts are the ways that God's love is shared.

Cut leaves for your tree from construction paper and let each family member write one item on each leaf that suggests something another person could do for them. Then place the leaves in a box or basket near the tree. During the week, let family members choose a leaf and complete the giving act. They can then tape the leaf to the tree branch of the appropriate person.

Day 20

"The King will reply, 'I tell you the truth, whatever you did for one of the least of these brothers of mine, you did for me.'"   Matthew 25:40

Sharing all that we have been given

After Jesus came and stayed at the house of Zacchaeus, a marvelous change took place in the tax collector's life. In Luke 19:8, Zacchaeus declares, "Look, Lord! Here and now I give half of my possessions to the poor, and if I have cheated anybody out of anything, I will pay back four times the amount." Jesus' presence called Zacchaeus to take stock of his life and his wealth. He considered the needs of others around him and offered to share his wealth with them.

As we assess all that we have, we should keep in mind those who do not have as much. We can ask Jesus to have the same presence in our lives as he did in the life of Zacchaeus. And out of the joy that comes from our relationship with Jesus, we can share our wealth, too. You and your family might consider making a special effort during Lent to share with others out of your abundance.

Abundance inventory

Take stock of your possessions and share with those less fortunate by taking an abundance inventory. Count how many of the following items you have in your household. Set aside the appropriate amount of money for each and give the money to a hunger relief fund or other charity. Talk about how much you have versus how much you need.

Television—25¢
VCR—25¢
CD player or stereo—25¢
Dishwasher—25¢
Car—10¢
Personal computer—25¢
Telephone—10¢
Lightbulbs—2¢
Rooms in your house—10¢ each
Toys—1¢ each

Videos—10¢ each
Winter coats—5¢
Shoes—2¢ a pair
Canned goods—1¢ each
Add your own categories and amounts!

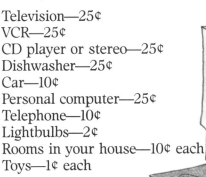

Day 21

"The King will reply, 'I tell you the truth, whatever you did for one of the least of these brothers of mine, you did for me.'" Matthew 25:40

Spring cleaning

In Italy, it is the custom at the end of the winter to burn the old "junk" that has accumulated throughout the year. As the entire community makes a pile of their junk, they gather around to watch as a straw witch *La Befana* is thrown on top of the pile to burn. *La Befana* is the "old lady of Epiphany" and she symbolizes the end of winter and the beginning of spring. Perhaps this is where the tradition of spring housecleaning first began!

Clean out your closets

Use this time to do some spring cleaning of your own. After everyone has sorted through their belongings, let them add them to boxes labeled "Keep," "Give," "Recycle," and "Repair." Choose one day to go together to give items to appropriate people or agencies and choose another day to work together to repair anything that needs it. An alternative is to hold a garage sale and donate the proceeds to charity.

Day 22

"The King will reply, 'I tell you the truth, whatever you did for one of the least of these brothers of mine, you did for me.'" Matthew 25:40

The legend of the robin and the thorns

Even though it was still midday, the sky on that first Good Friday had grown dark and ominous. The air was hot and still, and the birds in the treetops were silent.

One lone robin ventured forth to see what was happening. As it came near to Calvary, the robin saw Jesus on the cross. As the robin drew nearer, it saw that the crown of thorns Jesus was wearing had pierced the skin of his forehead. The robin felt sorry for the man upon the cross, and silently swooped down to pluck out the thorn. As the robin pulled the thorn clean, a drop of the blood from the wound fell upon the robin's breast, staining it blood red.

And to this day, the breast of the robin is red to remind us that a robin long ago tried to comfort Jesus as he suffered on the cross.

Caring for the birds

Birds are spoken of in many places in the Bible, and it is good for us to remember to care for all of God's creatures. Here are some ways that you can care for birds in your yard.

Make a simple bird bath from a sturdy log about 10-18" high. Square off the ends and then set the log on end in the lawn or near a flower garden. Put a terra cotta saucer on top of the log and keep it filled with fresh clean water. Scrub the saucer once a week to control the algae growth.

Create a special snack for the birds. Use a cookie cutter to cut into a slice of bread. Poke a hole in the top with a straw and brush the bread with egg white. Press birdseed onto the bread shape and let it dry. Thread a piece of yarn or string through the hole and hang it on a tree branch.

Day 23

"My eyes stay open through the watches of the night, that I may meditate on your promises. Hear my voice in accordance with your love; renew my life, O Lord, according to your laws." Psalm 119:148-149

Worried and distracted

We can learn a great lesson from the story of Jesus' visit with Mary and Martha (read Luke 10:38-42). As he came nearer to their home, Martha was probably putting the finishing touches on a good meal and was straightening up the house.

Even while Martha bustled about, Mary was waiting eagerly to hear the words Jesus had to teach them. And when he arrived, she sat listening to Jesus. Martha, on the other hand, complained to Jesus that Mary wasn't helping. " 'Martha, Martha,' the Lord answered, 'you are worried and upset about many things, but only one thing is needed. Mary has chosen what is better, and it will not be taken away from her' " (vv. 41-42).

Lent is a good time to slow down and reflect on what has priority in our lives. Are we like Martha, worried and upset, bustling around trying to do everything and resenting others for not pitching in? Perhaps we need to let go of some of those things that distract us from what is really important. Take Jesus' words to heart this week. Slow down and listen to God's Word.

What comes first?

One way to help your family to focus on those things that are most important is by taking a family priority inventory. Gather all family members together over a big bowl of popcorn and look closely at your engagement calendar. List all the week's upcoming events on a piece of paper. Then rank which are the most important to you. Decide as a group what activities might be skipped or postponed in order to have some family time. Be sure to schedule in a time for prayer and devotions each day. Close the time by reading together a favorite Bible story or sharing together in prayer.

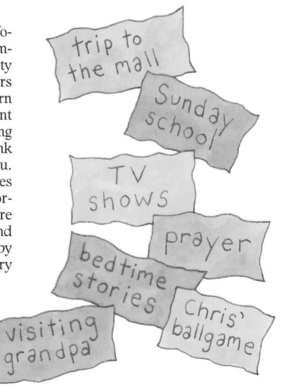

Day 24 ♪ HALLELUJAH! ♪

"My eyes stay open through the watches of the night, that I may meditate on your promises. Hear my voice in accordance with your love; renew my life, O Lord, according to your laws." Psalm 119:148-149

The story of Handel's *Messiah*

George Frederick Handel was one of the world's greatest composers. This story is told about him:

Handel was honored to be chosen by the king of England to compose a special oratorio. Wishing to please the king, Handel asked what kind of music he would like. The king replied, "Because it will be the Easter season, make it something set to verses from the Bible."

Handel set to work on the score. He practiced it over and over with the orchestra and chorus, making changes right up until the very night of the first performance.

Handel named the oratorio *Messiah,* a Hebrew word meaning "he who is an unexpected savior." One of the pieces in the work has become known as "The Hallelujah Chorus" be-

cause it uses the word *hallelujah*—"praise the Lord." It was with this piece that Handel was not satisfied. He wanted to end the chorus with a sound that was awesome and moving, but he just wasn't sure how to do it.

As he directed the chorus that night before the king, he was still not sure he had thought of the right way to express God's power and praise God's name. But as the chorus began, the king was so moved that he rose from his seat with tears streaming down his cheeks.

Because no one was supposed to remain seated if the king stood, everyone in the audience immediately stood up. The sound of everyone jumping to their feet had made the sensational sound that Handel had been trying to find!

Ever since that time, whenever *Messiah* is performed, it is traditional for everyone in the audience to stand as "The Hallelujah Chorus" begins.

Music and praise

Many great masterpieces of music have been composed for the glory of God. Check out from your local library recordings such as Handel's *Messiah* or Mahler's *Resurrection Symphony* or works by Bach or other great composers. Do some research on the backgrounds of these composers. Then turn your living room into a concert hall for an evening.

Often at Easter time, churches hold special concerts and performances that you may wish to attend together as a family.

Day 25

"My eyes stay open through the watches of the night, that I may meditate on your promises. Hear my voice in accordance with your love; renew my life, O Lord, according to your laws."   *Psalm 119:148-149*

The message of the psalms

The book of Psalms is a treasury of poetic hymns from the religious life of ancient Israel. Yet the psalms are not just ancient hymns; they continue to speak to the lives of people today. The book of Psalms offers us one of the best resources for devotion and meditation.

The book of Psalms can be a reservoir for our spiritual lives. As we read the ancient poetry, we can meditate on all that God has done. Like the psalmist, we can entreat God's mercy and rejoice in God's faithfulness. This Lenten season, take time to discover the rich depth of the psalms.

Expressions of faith

Poetry can be a means to express our thoughts, feelings, and ideas. As a family, try writing some poems that speak about your faith or the feelings you have about the seasons of Lent and Easter. One fun way to write poetry is in the form of an acrostic poem. Acrostic poems are based around a certain word. For example:

E arly on that bright morning,
A group of women approached the
    tomb.
S urprise!
T he tomb was empty!
E veryone was filled with wonder.
R ejoice! Jesus lives!

Choose a word and create your own acrostic poem. You might wish to write it on a piece of construction paper or poster board and illustrate it. Perhaps you could include it on an Easter card to send to friends and relatives.

Day 26

"My eyes stay open through the watches of the night, that I may meditate on your promises. Hear my voice in accordance with your love; renew my life, O Lord, according to your laws."   *Psalm 119:148-149*

Songs from the heart

Of all the types of hymns and music that Christians use in worship, perhaps the African American spirituals are most likely to be called songs from the heart. The words and melodies of these songs were born of slaves. They reflect the cries of anguish African Americans felt in their struggle for survival and freedom and the depth of their faith that God would deliver them. Sometimes the songs were sorrowful, not speaking of liberation but of survival amidst pain. One such song often sung during Lent is "Were You There?"

Were You There?

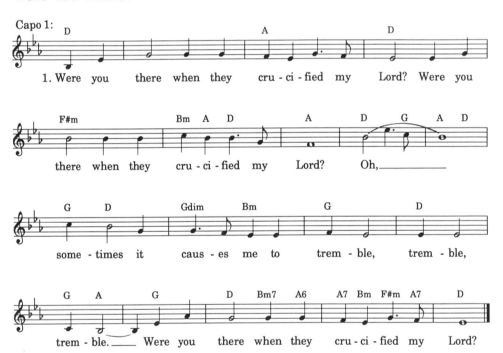

2. Were you there when they nailed him to the tree? . . .

3. Were you there when they laid him in the tomb? . . .

4. Were you there when God raised him from the tomb? . . .

40

Day 27

"My eyes stay open through the watches of the night, that I may meditate on your promises. Hear my voice in accordance with your love; renew my life, O Lord, according to your laws."   *Psalm 119:148-149*

Art as a reflection of faith

Visual art has been a part of the Christian church from its very beginnings. The earliest Christians lined the catacombs with paintings of Old Testament figures, martyrs, and apostles. Some of the paintings were crude, others were crafted by skillful artists. Yet all revealed a great commitment to witness to the suffering, death, and resurrection of Jesus. These pictures reflected a faith that stood strong in the face of persecution. They were portraits of hope.

Down through the ages, art has been used to inspire and encourage millions of Christians. Magnificent cathedrals have been built to the glory of God. Beautiful paintings have retold over and over the story of God's love. Our faith can be expressed in many ways—in pictures, in music, in words, and in loving deeds.

Paraffin prints

Supplies: One block of paraffin per design; blank paper (or notecards and envelopes); aluminum foil; iron; pencil; linoleum cutter; water-based printing ink; brayer or roller; spoon.

Use this art technique to make Easter cards to share with others. Let the cards celebrate the joyous resurrection of Jesus!

First, draw your card design on paper, reversing any letters or words so that they will read the right way when printed.

Smooth the surface of the paraffin block by covering it with foil and lightly running a warm iron over the block. Then transfer your design onto the wax, pressing hard with a dull pencil.

To print the cards, roll the brayer in the ink and then roll several times over the paraffin block. Lay the front of the notecard or folded paper on top of the block and press over the entire surface with the back of a spoon. Peel the paper away and let dry. Add your Easter greetings inside and send!

Day 28

"My eyes stay open through the watches of the night, that I may meditate on your promises. Hear my voice in accordance with your love; renew my life, O Lord, according to your laws."   *Psalm 119:148-149*

My remembrance

After Jesus ascended into heaven, the disciples were left to carry on the work of sharing the gospel with others. Although the newness of Jesus' teachings and the resurrection were closer to those disciples than they may seem to us, the words of the Bible are timeless.

Martin Luther said that Christians should remember their baptism each morning as they awaken, making the sign of the cross on their foreheads and offering a prayer of thanksgiving and dedication of the day to God. In this same way, Christians can remember the first Easter morning when Christ rose from the dead.

As you begin your day, why not try making the sign of the cross as a remembrance of the joy you have in the sure and certain hope of eternal life? Whether you make this sign before your feet touch the floor in the morning, before you eat breakfast, or even before you get into your car to drive to work or school, you will be making an intentional symbol that reminds you of God's work in your life.

Baptismal candle

If you have a candle from the service of your baptism, light it each year, or even each month on the anniversary of your baptismal date as a reminder of the light Jesus brings into your life. If you don't have a candle from this service, purchase or make a special candle you can use for this purpose.

Day 29

"Jesus took the Twelve aside and told them, 'We are going up to Jerusalem, and everything that is written by the prophets about the Son of Man will be fulfilled.'" Luke 18:31

The journey to the cross

We now enter the sixth week of Lent. The time for our spiritual journey is drawing to a close. Soon we will recount the activities of Jesus' last week before his crucifixion. In Luke 18:31-34, Jesus predicted his death. But his disciples did not understand Jesus' words. They did not know that the journey to Jerusalem would be the last that they took with Jesus. They only understood that they would accompany their teacher on a pilgrimage to the temple for the Passover.

We know from the Bible the events that took place in Jerusalem. We know that the journey for the disciples ended at the foot of the cross—or so they thought. Unlike the disciples, we can understand Jesus' words, "On the third day he will rise again" (v. 33). That truth makes the journey to the cross one of hope, not despair.

What do we take on our journey?

Most children enjoy taking a trip. They are easily caught up in the excitement of preparations and often want to help with the packing. This old parlor game reflects some of the fun of packing for a journey.

Have everyone sit in a circle. The leader begins by saying, "I am going on a journey. I will take along *(name some item)*." The person on the leader's left then repeats what the leader has said and adds one more item. Continue in this fashion around the circle. Whoever fails to name all the previous items drops out. Keep going around the circle until only one person remains.

You might add a new twist to the game by making it a faith journey. Start by saying "I am going on a journey. I am going to take along a loving spirit." Others might add things like patience, kindness, forgiveness, etc.

43

Day 30

"Jesus took the Twelve aside and told them, 'We are going up to Jerusalem, and everything that is written by the prophets about the Son of Man will be fulfilled.'"
Luke 18:31

The journeys of faith

The people of God have been a traveling people. The Bible records many different travels by many different modes of transportation—on the backs of animals, by foot on dusty roads, by chariot, by ship. Usually the journeys have started on a word from God:

"Go," said God to Abraham. "Go from your country to a land I will show you."

"Go to Pharaoh," God told Moses, "and tell him to let my people go."

"Go to Nineveh," God told Jonah, "and cry out against it."

"Get up," an angel of the Lord told Joseph, "and take the child and his mother and flee to Egypt."

"Follow me," called Jesus, "and I will make you fishers of men."

"Go and make disciples of all nations," proclaimed Jesus to his disciples.

These journeys all had one thing in common. They required faith on the part of the traveler that God would lead them and sustain them. And God did!

Bible journeys

Search your Bible for references to as many journeys as you can find. You might wish to make a contest of this among individual family members or teams. Use a concordance and look up words such as journey or travel. Here are a few references to get you started:

Luke 2:41-51
John 24:13-35
Acts 9:1-9
Acts 27:1-44

Day 31

"Jesus took the Twelve aside and told them, 'We are going up to Jerusalem, and everything that is written by the prophets about the Son of Man will be fulfilled.'" Luke 18:31

Jesus sends out his followers

When we go on a trip, we usually take along everything we will need. Occasionally we may forget a toothbrush, but it's not too difficult to pick up another as we travel. Few people would begin a journey without having packed anything.

In Luke 9:1-6 Jesus sent out his disciples to preach the kingdom of God and to heal the sick. He also instructed them to take nothing with them—no bags, food, money, or extra clothing! The disciples were to rely on the hospitality of those people they encountered. But there was no guarantee that the people would welcome them or their message. Sometimes we are called to go out in faith as the disciples did. Other times we are called to welcome those who come to us. We do it all in the name of Jesus.

Welcome mat

Supplies: Seagrass or sisal doormat; large plastic sewing needle; blue or green cotton fabric.

Make a welcome mat with a fish design to greet visitors to your home.

Cut fabric into 1" wide strips and use it to cross-stitch a pattern on the woven doormat. Follow the design as shown, tying on new fabric strips as needed.

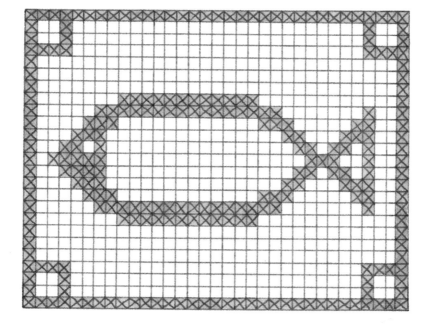

Day 32

"Jesus took the Twelve aside and told them, 'We are going up to Jerusalem. and everything that is written by the prophets about the Son of Man will be fulfilled.'"   *Luke 18:31*

Rocks in the way

Sometimes our journeys in life take us over rough paths where small stones get in our shoes and cause us discomfort. Other times we may have to crawl over larger rocks that block our way. But for the followers of Jesus, an even more formidable boulder appeared to stand in their way—the stone that sealed the entrance to Jesus' tomb. For the friends of Jesus, there was no way of getting around that rock. It was a symbol of death and despair.

But when the women approached the tomb early on the first Easter morning, to their amazement they found the stone rolled away! Jesus had risen! Their feet practically flew over the rocky path to tell the rest of the disciples. It's good to know that God can remove the biggest of obstacles!

Stone pendant

Supplies: a small stone; yarn or cord; scissors; white glue; paper cup; waxed paper; paintbrush.

Make a stone pendant to remind you that Jesus rose from the tomb and gives us the hope of new life.

Wash and dry your stone and place it in the center of a length of yarn or cording. Wrap the yarn around the stone, twisting the yarn in different directions. Tie the two ends of the yarn tightly at the top of the stone with a double knot.

Make a loop in the yarn by tying the two ends of the yarn into a second double knot a little higher than the first knot. Trim the ends of the yarn close to the second knot.

Pour a small amount of glue into the cup and place the stone onto a piece of waxed paper. Paint the stone and the yarn with a thin coating of the glue, being sure to keep the loop at the top open.

Let the glue dry, then slip a piece of yarn or cord through the loop. Knot the two ends of the yarn together to make a pendant.

Day 33

"Jesus took the Twelve aside and told them, 'We are going up to Jerusalem, and everything that is written by the prophets about the Son of Man will be fulfilled.'"   *Luke 18:31*

Colorful reminders of new life

In many homes, Easter is not complete without Easter eggs. But where did this colorful custom come from?

The symbol of the egg has its roots in pagan traditions. The Chinese, Egyptians, Greeks, Romans, and Persians celebrated the festival of Spring in honor of Eastre or Easter, the goddess of Spring. The egg was a symbol of the earth and the life that comes forth in springtime after a winter of barrenness. The Chinese are thought to be the first people to color eggs, dating back to 1000 B.C.

The tradition of hiding eggs developed much later, in Europe. Early folktales tell us that a German duchess decorated eggs and hid them in the tall grass. She invited children to find the eggs, and she told them that the eggs had been left by a rabbit. The Easter bunny still visits many countries today.

No longer are Easter eggs associated with festivals honoring a pagan goddess. Today they serve as colorful reminders of new life that comes with spring. If you choose to include Easter eggs in your observance of the season, talk with your family about other symbols that point to new life, especially the new life we have in Christ Jesus.

Glitter eggs

Supplies: Hard-boiled eggs; egg dyes; white glue; glitter; shallow dish.

Create beautiful eggs to decorate your home this Easter. Dye the eggs according to the directions on the egg dye. When they are dry, draw on symbols and designs with white glue and dip the egg in a shallow dish of glitter. Let the glue dry thoroughly before handling the eggs.

Day 34

"Jesus took the Twelve aside and told them, 'We are going up to Jerusalem, and everything that is written by the prophets about the Son of Man will be fulfilled.'"   Luke 18:31

The Faberge eggs

Peter Carl Faberge was a goldsmith who made the most beautiful jewelry that anyone had ever seen. Once, while on a trip to Paris, the Czar of Russia and his wife saw some of Faberge's work. The Czar's wife begged him to have Faberge make something for her, so the Czar himself went to talk with the goldsmith.

"I would like to make something for your wife," said Faberge. "But I have so much work to do it will take me at least three years before I can begin."

Usually, no one said no to the Czar. And the goldsmith could see how much the Czar loved his wife. "What would you like me to make, sir?" he said at last.

"Anything you like," the Czar replied. "But please have it ready for Easter."

In the year 1880, Faberge made a large white enamel egg. When the egg was opened, there was a yolk of pure gold inside. When the yolk was opened, there was a golden hen with ruby eyes. When you lifted the hen's beak, there was a tiny diamond crown inside that looked exactly like the crown of Russia—and from the crown hung a very small pendant made of rubies!

The Czar was amazed. As the years passed, he ordered 53 eggs from Faberge. Although ten are missing, we know there are still 43 of Faberge's eggs in existence today!

Rubber band resists

Supplies: Hard-boiled eggs; rubber bands of assorted widths; egg dyes.

Twist and wrap a variety of rubber bands around the egg, making sure the bands are snug. Dip into dye and let dry before carefully removing the rubber bands.

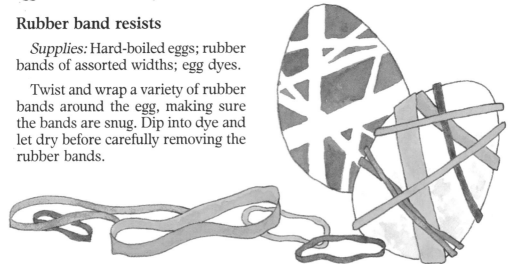

Palm Sunday (or Passion Sunday)

"Rejoice greatly, O Daughter of Zion! Shout, Daughter of Jerusalem! See, your king comes to you, righteous and having salvation, gentle and riding on a donkey, on a colt, the foal of a donkey." Zechariah 9:9

Celebrating Jesus' entry

Palm Sunday is celebrated on the Sunday before Easter. Another name for this Sunday is Passion Sunday, which changes the mood from one of triumph at Jesus' entry into Jerusalem, to one of somberness as the knowledge of the events of the coming week unfold.

The early Christians did not celebrate Palm Sunday until about the fourth century when worshipers began holding up olive twigs during the procession. The use of palms in the service did not begin until about 400 years later. By the tenth century, it was common practice to use palm branches in the processions, and they are still in use today.

The palm branches used in the service often are saved for use the following Ash Wednesday when they are burned for use in making ash crosses on worshipers' foreheads.

Palm frond crosses

Supplies: Fresh, moist palm fronds or green paper strips cut in ½" x 14" lengths.

Follow the diagrams to fold your palm leaves into a cross to display in your home until Easter.

① LAY THE ENDS OF TWO STRIPS ON TOP OF EACH OTHER TO FORM A RIGHT ANGLE AS SHOWN. FOLD 'A' DOWN, THEN BACK UP AROUND ITSELF TO MAKE A TIGHT LOOP AROUND 'B'.

③ SLIDE 'A' THROUGH THE CENTER IN BACK TO MAKE TOP OF CROSS. SLIDE 'B' THROUGH THE CENTER IN FRONT TO MAKE LEFT SIDE OF CROSS.

② FOLD 'B' BEHIND TO THE RIGHT, THEN THROUGH THE CENTER TO THE LEFT.

④ TO FINISH, TUCK THE ENDS OF 'A' AND 'B' INTO THE CENTER.

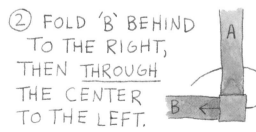

Day 35

"Jesus answered, 'I am the way and the truth and the life. No one comes to the Father except through me.' " *John 14:6*

Holy Week begins

After Jesus' jubilant entry into Jerusalem on Palm Sunday, the events leading toward Jesus' crucifixion began to unfold. The church calls this time Holy Week. On Monday and Tuesday of this week we recall how Jesus went to the temple in Jerusalem to teach the people for the last time. It was at that time that Jesus found the money-changers and merchants selling doves at exorbitant prices (see Mark 11:15-19).

When people questioned Jesus about who he was, they tried to trick him into saying things against the Roman government, but Jesus could not be tricked. Jesus used wisdom to answer the questions they asked him, and his enemies had to think of another way to get rid of him.

Symbols of Holy Week

The Christian church uses many symbols during Holy Week. Following is a list of symbols that relate to the events of Holy Week. See how many you and your family recognize, and use your Bible to locate and read about the others.

After reading about these symbols, you might want to plan a family scavenger hunt to see how many of them you can find. Make a display of the symbol objects you find for this holiest of weeks.

Torn curtain	Luke 23:44-46
Dice	Mark 15:24
Sponge and vinegar	John 19:28-29
Bowl and towel	John 13:3-17
Wooden cross	Mark 15:21
Alabaster vase	Mark 14:3-9
Nails	Luke 23:32-34
30 silver coins	Matt. 26:14-15
Thorn crown	Matt. 27:27-29
Palm branches	Matt. 21:8-9
Chalice	Luke 22:17-18
Grapes	Mark 14:23-25
Jug of wine	Luke 22:14-20
Loaf of bread	Luke 22:14-20
Unleavened bread	Matt. 26:17-29
Donkey	Matt. 21:1-3
Rock	Matt. 27:57— 28:2
Praying hands	Mark 14:32-36
Rooster	Mark 14:27-31

Day 36

"Jesus replied, ' "Love the Lord your God with all your heart and with all your soul and with all your mind." This is the first and greatest commandment. And the second is like it: "Love your neighbor as yourself." ' "

Matthew 22:37-38

The greatest commandment

As Holy Week continues, we read in the Bible how Jesus spent more time teaching the disciples and the crowds that followed him. He told the disciples many of the things that would happen in the coming days, but they did not always understand what he was saying to them.

Jesus told them about the greatest commandment, and how God wanted them to live. He also told his followers that he would come again in glory as the risen Christ.

Messages of love and joy

Supplies: Construction paper (assorted colors and white); pencil; crayons or felt-tip pens; cotton balls; scissors; glue; white acrylic paint.

Create cards to share with residents of a local nursing home or care center to brighten the lives of those who may not normally have many visitors.

Use white paper to make a bunny. With a pencil draw around your hand as shown, keeping your fingers together and your thumb pointing up. With pens or crayons draw on an eye, a nose, and a mouth under the thumb area. Add three lines for the whiskers. Color the inside of the ear pink. Then cut out the bunny shape.

Fold in half a piece of colored construction paper. Glue the bunny shape to the front. Glue on a cotton ball for the bunny's tail. Draw on a stem and branches for a pussy willow.

Dip your pinky in paint and print buds on the stem.

When the glue and paint dry, add a greeting inside: "All God's creatures want to wish you a happy Easter—including me!" or "May the love of Christ bloom in your life!"

Day 37

"He poured water into a basin and began to wash his disciples' feet, drying them with the towel that was wrapped around him. . . . When he had finished washing their feet, he put on his clothes and returned to his place. . . . 'I have set you an example that you should do as I have done for you.'"

John 13:5, 12, 15

The queen's foot washing

It was the custom in England that on Holy Thursday, the queen would wash the feet of as many beggars as she was years old, giving each of them one silver coin. In this way, the queen was following Jesus' example as recorded in John 13:4-15.

It is said that when the first Queen Elizabeth was 39 years old, she really didn't want to do the foot washing. She persuaded her lady-in-waiting to dress up as the queen and perform the ceremony instead.

As the lady-in-waiting began to wash the feet of the first few beggars, the real queen hid behind a curtain to watch. Now there was a young boy named Tom Gentry who was to have his feet washed. But he was so embarrassed that the queen would see his dirty feet that he ran behind the curtains to hide.

Whose arms did he run right into, but the queen's!

"Don't be ashamed, little boy," the queen said to Tom, "Your queen loves you!"

Then the Queen apologized to all the beggars for not washing their feet, and she washed Tom's feet herself. And she gave all the people *two* silver coins instead of just one.

An act of love and service

Talk about ways your family follows Jesus' example. When someone in your family is sick, how do you comfort and care for them? If a family member has a bad day, how does another person cheer them up?

Think of one way to share an act of love and service with another this week and do it secretly, remembering Jesus' words and following his example.

Day 38 (Maundy Thursday)

"And he took bread, gave thanks and broke it, and gave it to them, saying, 'This is my body given for you; do this in remembrance of me.' In the same way, after the supper he took the cup, saying, 'This cup is the new covenant in my blood, which is poured out for you.' "   Luke 22:19-20

Maundy Thursday

The Thursday before Easter has traditionally been called Maundy Thursday. The word *maundy* comes from the Latin word *mandatum*, meaning "commandment." The focus of this day is on the new commandment Jesus gave to his disciples to love one another as he loved them.

Maundy Thursday also recalls the last supper Jesus had with his disciples. We remember the last supper as the event when Jesus instituted Holy Communion. In many churches today, Communion is celebrated on Maundy Thursday.

The last supper took place during Passover, the commemoration of God's delivering the Hebrew people out of slavery in Egypt (Exodus 12). Passover is still observed by Jewish people the world over during a seven-day celebration. Part of the present-day Jewish Passover is the Seder, a special meal that came into practice more than 1000 years ago. Not to be confused with Communion, the Seder is a Jewish ritual. However, the Seder is a Jewish celebration of freedom that can help Christians understand Judaism and gain a deeper respect for our Old Testament roots.

Seder foods

The following are some foods used in a Seder. The *matzah* (unleavened bread) recalls how the people had to bake bread in haste before fleeing from Egypt. The *charoset* symbolizes the mortar they used in building while in captivity.

Matzah—Preheat the oven to 475°. Mix 3½ cups flour with 1 cup water and roll the dough onto a floured board. Transfer to a greased baking sheet. Score the large piece of dough into squares with a knife and poke holes in the pieces with the tines of a fork. Bake for 10-15 minutes or until golden brown. Cool and break into pieces.

Charoset—Mix together and serve as a salad: 6 medium apples, grated or finely chopped; ½ cup raisins; ½ teaspoon cinnamon; ¼ cup grape juice or wine; ½ cup chopped nuts.

Day 39 (Good Friday)

"When they came to the place called The Skull, there they crucified him, along with the criminals—one on his right, the other on his left. Jesus said, 'Father, forgive them, for they do not know what they are doing.'"

Luke 23:33-34

Good Friday

The Friday of Holy Week is called Good Friday, and it was most likely first known as "God's Friday." This day is a worldwide commemoration of Christ's suffering and death on the cross, and it has been remembered in that way since the fourth century.

Many cities sponsor processions through the streets on this day with singing and the carrying of heavy crosses to remember the pain and suffering of Jesus. The biggest procession always takes place in Jerusalem, along the path that Jesus is thought to have actually walked on his way to Calvary.

Churches often hold a service of *Tenebrae,* a "service of shadows" as they remember Jesus' last hours on the cross.

A service of shadows

Hold your own family service of shadows, using the candles on your Lenten wreath (pp. 6-7) as your only light. Begin with the candles lit. Have family members take turns reading the passages associated with the "shadows" and after each reading, extinguish one candle. When all candles have been extinguished, spend a moment in silent prayer before leaving the room quietly.

Shadow of betrayal
   Matthew 26:20-25
Shadow of inner agony
   Luke 22:40-44
Shadow of loneliness
   Matthew 26:40-45
Shadow of desertion
   Matthew 26:47-50, 55-56
Shadow of accusation
   Matthew 26:59-66
Shadow of mockery
   Mark 15:12-20
Shadow of death
   Luke 23:33-46

Day 40 (Holy Saturday)

"At the place where Jesus was crucified, there was a garden, and in the garden a new tomb, in which no one had ever been laid. Because it was the Jewish day of Preparation and since the tomb was nearby, they laid Jesus there."

John 19:41-42

The Easter vigil

The Saturday before Easter was a day of great sorrow for all of Jesus' followers. Their teacher and friend had died and been buried in a tomb, and because of the Jewish laws that forbade work on the Sabbath, they had not been able to prepare Jesus' body as they had hoped. Throughout this night, the first disciples kept a vigil as they waited for daybreak.

Today there are many people who observe an Easter vigil. They wait for the first light of dawn so that they too can experience the joy of the resurrection, just as the first disciples did when they discovered Jesus' body was gone from the tomb on the first Easter! Some of these vigils take place in churches that are dark, except for the burning of a single Paschal candle. As morning light comes, many candles are lit from this one bright light, symbolizing Jesus as the light of the world, who has forever conquered the dark night of sin.

A paschal candle

Supplies: One large white candle, at least 3″ in diameter; a stylus tool or skewer; felt-tip pen; five grains of clove or incense.

Make a paschal candle of your own to use during the Easter season.

Transfer some symbols of new life (pp. 21-22) onto the candle with a felt-tip pen. You could also use the first and last letters of the Greek alphabet—the *alpha* and the *omega*—to represent the beginning and the end. Include a cross in your design, to represent Christ.

After you have traced a design on the candle, use a stylus or skewer to carve the design into the wax. Insert the five cloves or grains of incense into the cross, one at each point and one in the center. These symbolize the wounds to his hands, feet, and side that Jesus received on the cross. You might also want to inscribe the date.

EASTER TO PENTECOST

Easter lasts more than one day. In fact, the season of Easter is celebrated from Easter Sunday to the Day of Pentecost, a week of weeks—fifty days in all! This time has come to be called The Great Fifty Days.

Easter is the oldest festival of the church year. The Great Fifty Days has been celebrated by the church much longer than some other liturgical seasons, like Advent and Lent. The season from Easter Sunday to Pentecost is celebrated as one long festival, although in the fourth century, another festival day was added—Ascension Day. Ascension Day comes toward the end of the Easter season, on the fortieth day, and it is generally considered part of the Easter celebration.

Unlike Christmas, Easter does not fall on the same day each year. Easter is always celebrated on a Sunday, but that Sunday can fall anywhere between March 22 and April 25.

Easter is a most joyful season. The color for Easter is white and the symbols associated with the season are beautiful and bright. Everything about the celebration points to the glorious resurrection of Jesus.

The Easter celebration reaches its culmination on the Day of Pentecost. On this major festival day, we celebrate the coming of the promised gift of the Holy Spirit. We rejoice that Jesus has risen and appeared to his disciples and has ascended to heaven. Now the coming of the Spirit gives the church the power and the necessary gifts to spread the good news to all the world. The color for the Day of Pentecost is red, symbolizing the fire of the Holy Spirit. The Day of Pentecost begins the longest season of the church year, extending until the first Sunday in Advent in December. The days following Pentecost are seen as a time for growth in the Spirit.

Easter Sunday

"On the first day of the week, very early in the morning, the women took the spices they had prepared and went to the tomb. They found the stone rolled away from the tomb, but when they entered, they did not find the body of the Lord Jesus. While they were wondering about this, suddenly two men in clothes that gleamed like lightning stood beside them. . . . The men said to them, 'Why do you look for the living among the dead? He is not here; he has risen!'"

Luke 24:1-6

The celebration begins!

Easter Sunday is the greatest Sunday of the church year, for without the resurrection, everything else would have no meaning. As such, it is welcomed with song and procession and joy by millions of people throughout the world. The days of fasting and reflection in Lent are over. The celebration is just starting!

Many churches begin their Easter celebrations with sunrise services. Like the women who visited the tomb early on that first Easter, we also can gather together at dawn to welcome the risen Lord. Sunrise services have long been held in the United States. The first of such services is thought to have taken place in Bethlehem, Pennsylvania, in 1741.

This year, your family may wish to rise early and attend a sunrise service. Or, you might hold a family service in your yard or in a favorite park at dawn. Follow it with a simple picnic breakfast and special prayers of thanksgiving for the new life Christ has brought to us.

An Easter egg tree

If you made a tree of Lenten symbols (p. 20), change it into an Easter egg tree today. Add yarn or ribbon to some eggs you have decorated and hang them from the tree. Blown eggs or plastic or foam eggs work well, since they are not as heavy as hard-boiled ones.

Bible verse egg hunt

Fill plastic eggs with scripture references related to the Easter story and hide them around the house or in your yard. After all the eggs have been found, look up the Bible verses and read them together.

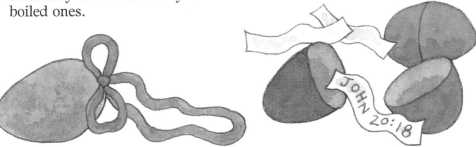

Second week of Easter

"They found the stone rolled away from the tomb."   *Luke 24:2*

Egg rolling at the White House

Dolly Madison was the wife of U.S. President James Madison. In 1814, she began the tradition of holding an Easter Monday egg rolling in Washington, D.C. Every year, hundreds of children brought their baskets full of decorated eggs to join the competition. The children rolled their eggs down the slopes near the Capitol, each hoping to be the one with an egg unbroken at the end of the race!

Then, in 1877, when President Rutherford B. Hayes was in office, a terrible thing happened. A new lawn was planted on the Capitol slopes, and the gardeners cancelled the yearly egg rolling!

The President's children, Fanny and Scott, begged their father to have the egg rolling anyway. But the gardeners refused. Finally the President's wife suggested that they hold the egg rolling on the lawns of the White House instead.

The President agreed, and ever since, on the Monday after Easter, the President's family invites hundreds of children to join in an egg rolling competition at the White House.

A family egg rolling

It has been said that egg rolling is symbolic of the stone being rolled away from the tomb. Whatever the origin of the custom, all will agree that it's fun!

Plan an egg rolling of your own. Invite several other families to join you, assigning a specific color egg to each family so you can keep track of the eggs as they roll. Set a course where there is a gently sloping lawn, and have fun!

Third week of Easter

"Then the two told what had happened on the way, and how Jesus was recognized by them when they broke the bread." Luke 24:35

On the road to Emmaus

It was evening on the first Easter. Two followers of Jesus were traveling to a village seven miles from Jerusalem. As they walked, a stranger joined them. The man listened as they recounted for him all that had happened that day—the open tomb, the words of the women who said they had seen angels, the missing body of Jesus. What did it all mean?

For some of the followers of Jesus, it was hard to believe the words of the women who went early to the tomb. They did not understand that Jesus was alive. They were wrapped up in their grief and their fear.

Even as the stranger spoke to the men on the road they did not recognize him. It was only when Jesus broke bread with them that they knew who their traveling companion was. Only then were they able to proclaim, "It is true! The Lord has risen!"

Eggshell mosaics

Supplies: Eggshell pieces in a variety of colors; poster board; white glue; pencil; scissors.

Use the shells from your Easter eggs to make colorful mosaics that symbolize how through Christ our lives have been put back together!

Cut the poster board into 9" x 12" pieces. Lightly sketch your mosaic design on the poster board. When pleased with the design, spread a thin layer of white glue in one color space at a time and fill in with eggshells. Repeat for all the colors until the design is complete. Let dry and then display your new creation.

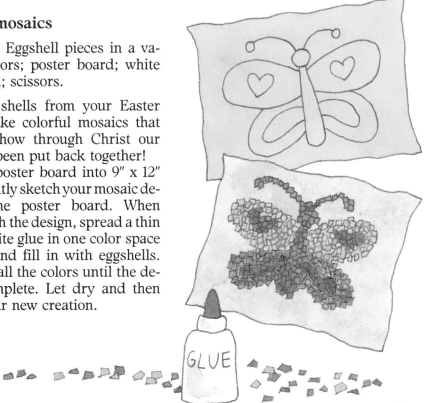

Fourth week of Easter

"Praise be to the God and Father of our Lord Jesus Christ! In his great mercy he has given us new birth into a living hope through the resurrection of Jesus Christ from the dead."   *1 Peter 1:3*

New life springs forth

An Easter hymn entitled "Now the Green Blade Rises" recalls how like the wheat that sprouts from seed buried deep in the earth, Jesus rose from the dead to bring us new life. Each year, as the ground thaws and green plants emerge, we witness the signs of new life in nature. With Easter, we also claim the promise of new life in Christ. Because of God's great mercy, we have a living hope. Hallelujah!

Seed scope

Supplies: Clear glass or jar with straight sides, at least 4″ tall; 2 pieces of dark construction paper; paper towels; 4-5 large seeds, such as corn or lima beans; water.

Line the inside of the jar with one piece of construction paper. Crumple paper towels and fill the inside of the jar with them. Slip the seeds, evenly spaced, between the jar and the construction paper, about 1½″ below the rim. Carefully add water so that the toweling soaks up the water and wets the construction paper as well. Wrap a second piece of construction paper around the outside of the jar and set the seed scope in a sunny window.

Remove the cover each day to check the progress of the seeds. Add water daily to keep the towels damp. The seeds should soon swell and sprout. When the plants are about 4″ high, transplant them to a container of soil.

Fifth week of Easter

"See! The winter is past; the rains are over and gone. Flowers appear on the earth; the season for singing has come."   Song of Songs 2:11-12

Flowers of spring

How beautiful are the flowers that bloom in the spring! Their bright colors warm our hearts and bring joy to our lives. In these days following Easter Sunday our prayers are ones of praise and our songs are filled with thanksgiving to our God who makes all things new.

Share the good news of Easter with others this week. You might visit someone who is homebound, taking along a gift of flowers to brighten their home. Or send someone far away a special greeting and let the person know that you are including him or her in your prayers this week.

A basket of joy

Supplies: Construction paper, wrapping paper, or wallpaper remnants; pencil; scissors; glue; paper lace doily; fresh, dried, or silk flowers; ribbon.

Enlarge the cone shape for the basket. Cut out as indicated by the solid lines and fold on the dotted line. Run a thin layer of glue along the folded edge and roll into a cone. Hold for several seconds until the glue sets.

Insert the paper doily into the cone. Glue on a ribbon handle and fill with flowers.

GLUE HERE

Sixth week of Easter

"And I will ask the Father, and he will give you another Counselor to be with you forever—the Spirit of truth. . . . I will not leave you as orphans; I will come to you. Before long, the world will not see me anymore, but you will see me. Because I live, you also will live."   John 14:16-19

We have Jesus' word

Before ascending to his Father, Jesus promised he would return. The following story illustrates the trust we have in that promise from Jesus.

Before a young man left for a long journey he handed a letter to the woman he intended to marry. "It is a pledge of my honor and love," the young man assured her.

Days turned into months and months into years, but the young woman never heard from her beloved. As time passed she became more and more depressed. Her friends urged her to forget the traveler and begin to see other men. She steadfastly refused.

One day while looking through her desk she discovered the letter her beloved had left her. She read it slowly and her spirits lifted. In the days ahead she reread the letter many times. It gave her comfort.

Finally, after many years the young man returned home. "I am grateful, but amazed, that you are still waiting for me. How was it possible for you to remain faithful during my long absence?" he asked.

"Even you don't understand?" the young woman said. "I believed in you because I had your word, in the letter."

Rejoice windsock

Supplies: Plastic 5-quart ice cream bucket; permanent felt-tip markers; crepe paper streamers or wide ribbon; wide plastic tape; scissors.

Make and fly this colorful windsock as a reminder of the joy we have in knowing Jesus will return.

Cut the bottom off the bucket. Write REJOICE in large letters around the bucket with a permanent marker. Cut 12 streamers, 24" long. Evenly space the streamers around the bottom of the bucket and attach with plastic tape.

Seventh week of Easter

"But you will receive power when the Holy Spirit comes on you; and you will be my witnesses in Jerusalem, and in all Judea and Samaria, and to the ends of the earth." Acts 1:8

The celebration continues

With these words of Jesus (Acts 1:8), the first disciples learned that Easter was not the end, but the beginning. Even though after Jesus spoke these words he was taken up to heaven, the disciples knew they were not abandoned. The Holy Spirit was coming to them, and they would receive what was needed to continue to share the story of God's salvation with the world. As Jesus' words encouraged the disciples in their day to continue to spread the good news, may you also be encouraged and guided by the Spirit in sharing this story through your words and your lives!

Good news kite

Supplies: Paper grocery bag; string; hole punch; felt-tip markers.

To celebrate Jesus' ascension, spend an afternoon flying kites.

A simple kite can be made from a large grocery sack. Punch holes in the four corners at the top of the bag. Attach 18″ long strings to each corner and knot the strings together. Tie a long string to the knot for flying. Decorate the bag with designs and words that proclaim the Easter gospel and send the message aloft. Note: The kite works best if the kite flyer is running with it!

The Day of Pentecost

"When the day of Pentecost came, they were all together in one place. Suddenly a sound like the blowing of a violent wind came from heaven and filled the whole house where they were sitting. They saw what seemed to be tongues of fire that separated and came to rest on each of them. All of them were filled with the Holy Spirit and began to speak in other tongues as the Spirit enabled them."
Acts 2:1-4

The coming of the Holy Spirit as wind

Throughout his ministry Jesus had told the disciples about the gift of the Holy Spirit: the helper, the comforter who would come to them after Jesus had returned to heaven. Imagine the excitement of the disciples at Pentecost when they were actually able to understand about this great gift Jesus had told them about!

The wind is something we cannot see. But we *can* see the effects the wind has on other things. So at times it seems to be with the gift of the Holy Spirit in our lives.

Wind spinners

Supplies: Construction paper; scissors; paper clip; pen.

As a reminder of the Holy Spirit in your life, make wind spinners.

Cut a large flame shape from construction paper. Then cut the shape in a spiral fashion, beginning at the outer edge as shown. Write the words "Blow, Spirit!" along the spiral. Hold the center section and let the rest of the spiral drop down. Attach a paper clip to the center piece for hanging.

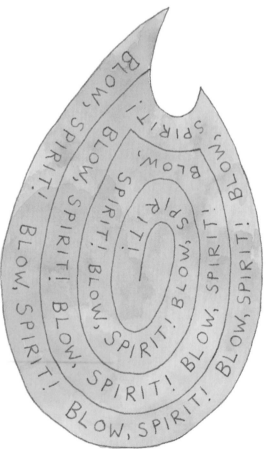